HTML

FOR

BEGINNERS

1st Edition

By Ganofins

Published by Ganofins

About the Author

Ganesh Bagaria who is known by his online alias **Ganofins** is the owner of Worldfreeapps.com website. At present he is a college student and he lives in India. Worldfreeapps is a website for downloading Android Apps and Games or Apks.

You can connect to **Ganofins** on his YouTube channel and on other social sites

BECOME A GANOFINIAN ► ► http://bit.ly/BecomeAGanofinian

Socials:-

Facebook ► https://www.facebook.com/Ganofins

Twitter   ► https://twitter.com/ganofins

Instagram ► https://instagram.com/ganofins

Tumblr   ► http://ganofins.tumblr.com

Index

Introduction

Welcome to HTML for Beginners by Ganofins in which you know everything about the HTML.

HTML stands for Hyper Text Markup Language. Which is used on web to develop web pages.

HTML was created by Berners-Lee in late 1991 but HTML 2.0 was the first standard HTML specification which was published in 1995. And then HTML 4.01 was published in 1999 and then HTML 5 in 2012.

To create HTML documents you will need text editors like notepad, notepad++, simple text editor etc.

You will need a web browser like Google Chrome, Internet Explorer, or Mozilla Firefox etc. to see the preview of that HTML document which you have created.

As HTML is a markup language and makes use of various tags to format the content and these tags are enclosed within angle braces **<Tag Name>**.

HTML Document Structure

A simple HTML document will have following structure:-

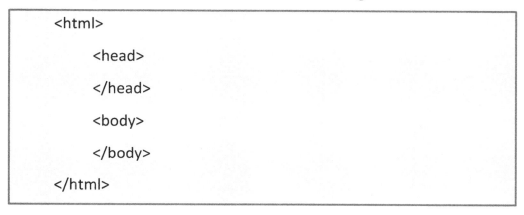

```
<html>
        <head>
        </head>
        <body>
        </body>
</html>
```

In between the **<head>…. </head>** tag Document header related tags are added.

In between the **<body>…. </body>** tag Document body related tags are added.

We will study the header and body tags in details in subsequent pages.

First HTML Webpage

```html
<html>

<head>

<title>HTML for Beginners

</title>

</head>

<body>

<p>A book by Ganofins (Ganesh Bagaria).</p>

</body>

</html>
```

When you run your above HTML document in browser than you will get this result.

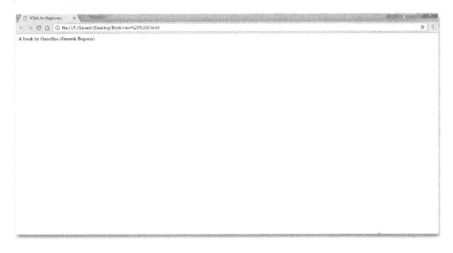

HTML Tag

HTML Document starts with **<html>** tag and ends with **</html>** tag.

This tag encloses the complete HTML document and mainly comprises of document header which is represented by **<head>…. </head>** and document body which is represented by **<body>…. </body>** tags.

And the **<!DOCTYPE>** Declaration tag is also added in HTML document to tell web browser about the HTML version. And currently the HTML version is 5.0.

The ability to code using HTML is essential for any web professional.

Example:

```
<html>

        ………………

</html>
```

Head, Title Tags

Head Tag: Head tag represents the document's header which can keep other HTML tags like <title>, <link> etc. Or the head of an HTML file contains all of the non-visual elements that help make the page work.

Example:

```
<html>
  <head>….. </head>
</html>
```

Title Tag: Title tag is added inside the <head> tag to mention the document title.

Example:

```
<html>
  <head>
    <title>HTML for Beginners</title>
  </head>
</html>
```

Body Tag

The **<body>** tag follows the head tag. It represents the document's body which keeps other HTML tags like <h1>, <div>, <p>, <a>, <img> etc. And it contains all visual-structural elements.

Example:

```
<html>

  <head>…. </head>

  <body>

  …..

  </body>

</html>
```

So, we put every tag enclosed between the body tags.

Headings and Paragraphs

Headings: HTML includes six level of headings, which are ranked according to their importance. These are <h1>, <h2>, <h3>, <h4>, <h5> and <h6>.

While displaying any heading, browser adds one line before and one line after that heading.

Example:

```
<html>
   <head>…. </head>
   <body>
      <h1>HTML for Beginners</h1>
      <h2>HTML for Beginners</h2>
      <h3>HTML for Beginners</h3>
      <h4>HTML for Beginners</h4>
      <h5>HTML for Beginners</h5>
      <h6>HTML for Beginners</h6>
   </body>
</html>
```

Paragraphs: Paragraph tag is represented by <p>. It offers a way to structure your text into different paragraphs. Each paragraph is typed between opening tag **<p>** and closing tag **</p>.**

Example:

```
<html>
  <head>…. </head>
  <body>
    <p>A book by Ganofins</p>
    <p>A book by Ganofins</p>
  </body>
</html>
```

Text Formatting

1. **Bold: \...** tag is used to make the text bold in HTML.

Example:

```
<html>
  <head>.... </head>
  <body>
    <p><b>A book by Ganofins</b></p>
  </body>
</html>
```

2. **Italic: \<i>...\</i>** tag is used to make or to display the text as Italic on the web page.

Example:

```
<html>
  <head>.... </head>
  <body> <p><i>A book by Ganofins</i></p> </body>
</html>
```

3. Underline: <u>...</u> tag is used to appear the text as underlined in the webpage.

Example:

```
<html>
  <head>.... </head>
  <body>
    <p><u>A book by Ganofins</u></p>
  </body>
</html>
```

4. Centre: <center>...</center> tag is used to display the text in centre on the webpage.

Example:

```
<html>
  <head>.... </head>
  <body>
    <p><center>A book by Ganofins</center></p>
  </body> </html>
```

5. Marquee: \<marquee>...\</marquee> tag is used to move the text or image or video in the webpage.

Example:

```
<html>
  <head>…. </head>
  <body>
    <p><marquee>A book by Ganofins</marquee></p>
  </body>
</html>
```

6. Quotation: \<q>...\</q> tag is used to add quotation marks in the sentence.

Example:

```
<html>
  <head>…. </head>
  <body>
    <q>THANKS FOR READING</q>
  </body> </html>
```

7. Break: **\
** is used to break the line.

Example:

```
<html>
  <head>…. </head>
  <body>
    <p>A book by Ganofins</p><br>
    <p>THANKS FOR READING</p>
  </body>
</html>
```

8. Superscript: \[…] tag is used to make the text appear as super script in the webpage.

Example:

```
<html>
  <head>…. </head>
  <body>
    <p>A book by <sup>Ganofins</sup></p>
  </body> </html>
```

9. Subscript: **_{...\}** tag is used to make the text appear as subscript in the webpage.

Example:

```
<html>
  <head>.... </head>
  <body>
    <p>A book by<sub> Ganofins</sub></p>
  </body>
</html>
```

10. Strikeout: **\<strike>...\</strike>** tag is used to make text strikeout.

Example:

```
<html>
  <head>.... </head>
  <body>
    <p>A book by<strike> Ganofins</strike></p>
  </body> </html>
```

11. Deleted Text: <del>...</del> is used to display the text as deleted.

Example:

```
<html>
  <head>…. </head>
  <body>
    <p>A book by<del> Ganofins</del></p>
  </body>
</html>
```

Attributes

An attribute is used to define the characteristics of an HTML element and is placed inside the element's opening tag.

Attributes names and attribute values are case-insensitive.

1. **Align:** align attribute is used to align the object horizontally.

Example:

```
<html>
  <head>…. </head>
  <body>
    <p align="right">A book by Ganofins</p>
    <p align="left">A book by Ganofins</p>
    <p align="center">A book by Ganofins</p>
  </body>
</html>
```

2. Valign: It is used to align the object vertically in the HTML page.

Example:

```
<html>
  <head>…. </head>
  <body>
    <p align="top">A book by Ganofins</p>
    <p align="middle">A book by Ganofins</p>
    <p align="bottom">A book by Ganofins</p>
  </body>
</html>
```

3. bgcolor: This attribute place a background colour behind an element.

Example:

```
<html>
  <head>…. </head>
  <body bgcolor="red">
    <p>A book by Ganofins</p>
  </body>
</html>
```

4. **background:** It is used to add a background image behind an element.

Example:

```
<html>
  <head>…. </head>
  <body background="ganofinians.jpg">
    <p>A book by Ganofins</p>
  </body>
</html>
```

5. **Id:** It names an element for use with CSS.

Example:

```
<html>
  <head>…. </head>
  <body>
    <p id="ganofins">A book by Ganofins</p>
    <p id="ganofinians">THANKS FOR READING</p>
  </body>
</html>
```

6. **Width:** width attribute specifies the width of the table, image, etc.

Example:

```
<html>
  <head>…. </head>
  <body>
    <img src="ganofins.jpg" width="75%">
  </body>
</html>
```

7. Height: height attribute specifies the height of the table, image, etc.

Example:

```
<html>
  <head>…. </head>
  <body>
    <img src="ganofins.jpg" height="75%">
  </body>
</html>
```

Images

Without images your webpage may seems boring so to add Image in your webpage.

<img> tag is used to add image and it has no closing tag.

Example:

```
<html>
  <head>…. </head>
  <body>
    <img src="ganofins.jpg" height="75%" width="75%"
alt="Hello Ganofinians!">
  </body>
</html>
```

- In "src" attribute we add our image's location or the path of the image.

- About "height" and "width" I already taught you.

- "Alt" attribute specifies an alternative text for an image, if the image cannot be displayed.

Links

Links allows people to go through different webpages. You can create hyperlink in text, image, sentence, etc.

<a href="Document URL"></a> tag is used to make text, image, etc. linkable

Example:

```
<html>
  <head>…. </head>
  <body>
    <p><a href="http://bit.ly/BecomeAGanofinian"
target="_blank">Ganofins Channel</a></p>

    <p><a href="http://bit.ly/BecomeAGanofinian"
target="_self">Ganofins Channel</a></p>

    <p><a href="http://bit.ly/BecomeAGanofinian"
target="_parent">Ganofins Channel</a></p>

    <p><a href="http://bit.ly/BecomeAGanofinian"
target="_top">Ganofins Channel</a></p>

  </body>
</html>
```

- "_blank" Opens the linked document in a new window or tab.

- "_self" Opens the linked document in the same frame.

- "_parent" Opens the linked document in the parent frame.

- "_top" Opens the linked document in the full body of the window.

Address

<address>...</address> tag is used to add signature block for webpage.

Example:

```
<html>
  <head>…. </head>
  <body>
    <address>Ganofins</address>
  </body>
</html>
```

Lists

List can be created in the Webpage. <li>...<li> tag is used to add a list item in the list.

There are two types of list:-

1. **Ordered List (<ol>...</ol>):** If this tag is used then your list will be displayed in the numerical or alphabetical order.

Example:

```
<html>
  <head>.... </head>
  <body>
    <ol>
      <li>HTML</li>
      <li>MySQL</li>
    </ol>
  </body>
</html>
```

2. Unordered list (<ul>...</ul>): If this tag is used then your list will be displayed in an unordered way means in Bullets form.

Example:

```
<html>
  <head>.... </head>
  <body>
    <ul>
      <li>HTML</li>
      <li>MySQL</li>
    </ul>
  </body>
</html>
```

Tables

<table>...</table> tag is used to create table. Let's see an example and then I will explain it:-

Example:

```
<html>
  <head>.... </head>
  <body>
    <table bgcolor="red" border="2" align="center">
      <tr>
        <td>HTML</td>
        <td>MySQL</td>
      </tr>
    </table>
  </body>
</html>
```

- <tr>...</tr> tag means table row which adds a row in the table.

- <td>...</td> tag means table data in which you add the data of the table.

- "bgcolor" attribute is used to add background colour in the table.

- "align" attribute is used to change the horizontal position of the table in webpage.

- "border" attribute is used to add the border in the table. Without border there is meaning of the table.

THANKS FOR READING THE BOOK

Check out my another book

MySQL for Beginners:- https://www.amazon.com/MySQL-Beginners-Ganofins-ebook/dp/B01028DQZU

You can connect to me **Ganofins** on my YouTube channel and on other social sites

BECOME A GANOFINIAN ▶ ▶ http://bit.ly/BecomeAGanofinian

Socials:-

Facebook ▶ https://www.facebook.com/Ganofins

Twitter   ▶ https://twitter.com/ganofins

Instagram ▶ https://instagram.com/ganofins

Tumblr   ▶ http://ganofins.tumblr.com

www.ingramcontent.com/pod-product-compliance
Lightning Source LLC
Chambersburg PA
CBHW022312070326
40689CB00049BA/1355